YOUR PET HAMSTER

A TRUE BOOK

by
Elaine Landau

Children's Press®
A Division of Grolier Publishing

New York London Hong Kong Sydney
Danbury, Connecticut

Reading Consultant
Linda Cornwell
Learning Resource Consultant
Indiana Department
of Education

Author's Dedication:
For Jerry, Bianca,
and Abraham

A hamster
in a teacup

Library of Congress Cataloging-in-Publication Data

Landau, Elaine
  Your pet hamster/ by Elaine Landau.
    p.   cm. — (A True book)
  Includes bibliographical refernces (p.) and index.
  Contents: Hamsters as pets — Picking out your pet — Your Hamster's
home — Hamsters at play — Feeding — A healthy hamster — You and
your hamster.
    ISBN 0-516-20383-5 (lib.bdg.)   0-516-26265-3(pbk.)
    1. Hamsters as pets—Juvenile literature. [1. Hamsters. 2. Pets] I. Title.
II. Series.
SF459.H3L35 1997
636.9'356—dc21   97-15625
                                                  CIP
                                                  AC

© 1997 Children's Press®, a Division of Grolier Publishing Co., Inc.
All rights reserved. Published simultaneously in Canada.
Printed in the United States of America.
1 2 3 4 5 6 7 8 9 0 R 06 05 04 03 02 01 00 99 98 97

Contents

Some people think hamsters make perfect pets.

Hamsters As Pets

Is a hamster the perfect pet for you? It just might be. To begin with, hamsters are larger than mice, and many people think they're cuter. They are also naturally clean animals.

Hamsters, and the equipment needed to keep them, are fairly inexpensive compared to other pets. They are not noisy animals, and their small size makes them ideal if you live in a small house or an apartment. Hamsters store dry food in their cages, so a family can safely leave their hamster alone for a weekend. You won't need to have someone stop by to feed it.

New hamster owners are usually delighted with their pets. Tame hamsters like to be held. They are curious,

A hamster's small size means it can live happily in small houses or apartments.

Tame hamsters like to be held.

active creatures and are fun to watch as they climb and scamper about. Of all the small animals sold in pet shops, many people think hamsters make the perfect pets.

Hamsters are naturally curious.

A Hamster For Everyone

Hamsters come in a wide variety of colors, such as beige, cream, and white. They can be many different sizes, and there are long-haired and short-haired hamsters. Choose the type you like best.

Picking Out Your Pet

You can buy a hamster in a pet store. Look for a clean store where the animals are well cared for. Don't be afraid to ask the salesperson questions about hamster care. You want to be a responsible pet owner, and the salespeople are there to help you.

Buy a hamster from a clean pet store where the animals are well cared for.

Hamsters do not
like the company of
other hamsters.

Some small rodents are extremely social and do well in pairs. But this is not true of hamsters in the wild. Hamsters prefer to live alone. They spend only a short time with other hamsters. If two hamsters are kept in a small cage, brutal fights are likely to break out.

Healthy hamsters are active little creatures with bright, clear eyes and hairy ears that stand straight up. Their bodies

A healthy hamster's ears stand up.

are well rounded, and their coats are shiny.

Pass up any hamster with a runny nose, an injured limb, bald spots, or a thin coat. A hamster has a life span of only two to three years, so do not buy a pet that is more than twelve weeks old.

Look for a hamster with a well-rounded body and a shiny coat.

Hamster Cage

You'll need a container or cage for your hamster to live in. Most pet stores that sell hamsters also carry these cages. Hamster homes made of stainless steel or plastic with wire mesh covers are popular. A large birdcage or fish aquarium is also suitable. Some types of hamster homes have colored, see-through tubes connected in various ways.

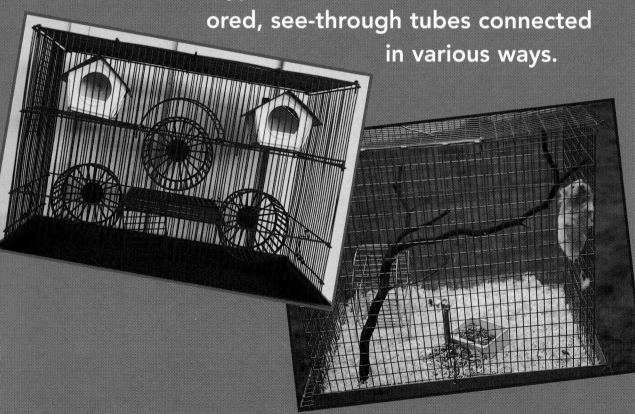

Roundup

They are designed to make the animal feel as though it is living in an underground burrow.

When you buy your hamster's home, think big. Hamsters are tiny animals, but they love to explore and play. Keeping a hamster in a small container without room to move about is like putting it in a prison.

Your Hamster's Home

No matter what type of cage you get, it's important to keep your pet's living space both safe and sanitary.

Clean your hamster cage thoroughly once a week. Use a mild disinfectant to scrub the cage. Rinse and dry the cage carefully before you put your hamster back in it.

Wood shavings make excellent bedding. A hamster will burrow in the bedding and make a place to sleep.

You will need to furnish your hamster's home. Start by spreading a layer of bedding 1 to 2 inches (2.5 to 5 cm) deep over the entire cage

Hamsters will store food in the bedding.

floor. Bags of wood shavings are sold in pet stores. This material is a fine, low-cost bedding choice.

Some people use hay for their hamster's bedding, but

it's not a good idea. Hay often carries dirt, and your hamster would breathe it in. Hay may also contain tiny insects that carry disease, such as mites.

Replace all the bedding every week when you clean out your hamster's cage. Hamsters usually make a toilet area in the corner of their cage farthest from where they sleep. Remove the soiled bedding in this area every two to three days.

Hamsters at Play

Hamsters love toys, and it's delightful to watch them play. They especially enjoy climbing. If its cage has horizontal bars, your pet will climb on them. You can also buy small hamster ladders. Many people find that hamsters like to climb on small wooden branches and

Hamsters love to climb. Branches make excellent additions to a hamster's home.

twigs attached to their cage. To avoid injuries, check these branches every few days to make sure they are still secure.

Hamsters also use branches to sharpen their claws and to gnaw on. So only take branches from nonpoisonous trees that have not been sprayed with a toxic insect repellent. Before you put a branch into the cage, wash it thoroughly with hot water and allow it to dry.

Hamsters love exercise wheels, and these often come attached to the hamster cages sold in pet stores. Some hamsters run 4 to 8 miles (6 to 13 km) a night on these wheels.

Some hamsters run
many miles each night
on exercise wheels.

Hamsters will explore new objects in their cages.

You can buy a variety of hamster toys. Just make sure that the ones you pick are made of nontoxic materials and have no sharp edges.

Your hamster will also enjoy the "free" toys you can find around the house. Cardboard egg cartons and tubes from toilet paper and paper towel rolls are great favorites.

Many household objects make great hamster toys.

Feeding

Pet stores sell dry hamster food mixtures that contain nuts, grains, seeds, and other healthful ingredients. These mixtures are probably the best basic food for your pet.

Hamsters need other foods as well. Daily feedings of small amounts of fruits and

Hamster food mixtures (top) contain healthful ingredients for your pet. Hamsters also enjoy small amounts of fruits and vegetables (bottom left and right).

vegetables add variety and fluids to your pet's menu. Most hamsters like carrots, potatoes, apples, and lettuce (use lettuce in very small amounts). You can also include some live crickets and a bit of the pellet food made especially for small animals.

You will need feeding tools for your hamster. Pick a food dish that is easy to clean. Make sure it is heavy enough not to be tipped over by your pet.

Choose a food dish that will not easily tip over.

Hamsters are hoarders. They like to store food. They fill their cheek pouches with food and then hide it in their cages for later. While you want to keep your pet's cage clean, do not continually remove the hoarded food. That would upset the animal. But don't feed your pet large amounts of any food that spoils quickly.

Hamsters were originally desert animals, so they need very little water. They get most of the water they need from the food they eat, but you should always make fresh water available to your pet. You can buy a water bottle made for hamsters and rats at

A hamster drinks from a bottle with a steel spout.

your pet store. These bottles come with a drinking tube so you can be sure you are giving your pet clean water. A bottle with a stainless-steel spout will best withstand a hamster's gnawing.

A Healthy Hamster

Hamsters are small but hardy creatures. With the proper diet and a clean home, they are likely to stay healthy.

Keep your hamster's cage in a draft-free area out of direct sunlight. And try not to expose your pet to extreme differences in temperature.

Hamsters are hardy animals.

Because hamsters are most active at night, they need quite a bit of rest during the day. Do not continually disrupt your pet's sleep. A hamster

Hamsters need time to sleep during the day.

that is not well rested will have a shortened life span.

If your hamster becomes ill, take it to a veterinarian. If you treat your pet with a home remedy, you might do more harm than good.

You and Your Hamster

Hamsters are naturally playful creatures. They enjoy being around people they know and trust. But a shocked, fearful, or angry hamster might nip your fingers.

So let your pet get to know you before you try to pick it up. After it has become used

Hamsters are playful creatures.

Once a hamster has gotten to know you, it will like to be held.

to seeing you and hearing your voice, you can extend your hand into its cage.

Hamsters enjoy being out of their cages for an hour or two at a time. They like to move about freely in a large space and explore new areas.

Before you let your hamster out, be sure the door to the room is tightly closed—you don't want your hamster to travel farther than expected. Also, keep larger pets that could harm the hamster out of the room.

Hamsters are interesting
and amusing pets. They
deserve caring and responsible owners.

Be a caring and
responsible
hamster owner.

To Find Out More

Here are some additional resources to help you learn more about hamsters:

 **Books**

Chrystie, Frances. **Pets: A Comprehensive Handbook for Kids.** Little, Brown, 1995.

Hansen, Elvig. **Guinea Pigs.** Carolrhoda Books, 1992.

King-Smith, Dick. **I Love Guinea Pigs.** Candlewick Press, 1995.

Petty, Kate. **Hamsters.** Franklin Watts, 1991.

Sproule, Ann. **Hamsters.** Bookwright Press, 1988.

Wexler, Jerome. **Pet Hamsters.** Whitman, 1992.

Ziefert, Harriet. **Let's Get A Pet.** Viking, 1993.

Organizations and Online Sites

Acme Pet
http://www.acmepet.com/

Includes useful information on all kinds of animals.

American Society for the Prevention of Cruelty to Animals (ASPCA)
424 East 92nd Street
New York, NY 10128-6804
(212) 876-7700, ext. 4421
http://www.aspca.org/

This organization is dedicated to the prevention of cruelty to animals. They also provide advice and services for caring for all kinds of animals.

Petstation
http://petstation.com/

An online service for pet owners and anyone interested in animals. Includes resources for kids.

Pet Talk
http://www.zmall.com/pet/

An online resource of animal care information.

Important Words

aquarium glass tank in which fish, small animals, or plants may be kept

disinfectant chemical substance that destroys harmful bacteria

hardy strong

hoard to store something for later use

nontoxic not poisonous

pellet a hard round ball

remedy to cure or heal

rodent one of a group of small, gnawing animals

sanitary free of dirt and germs

species a specific type of plant or animal

veterinarian doctor who treats animals

Index

Meet the Author

Elaine Landau worked as a newspaper reporter, children's book editor, and youth services librarian before becoming a full time writer. She has written more than ninety books for young people.

Ms. Landau lives in Florida with her husband and son.

Photo Credits ©: Ben Klaffke: 11, 13, 18, 21, 22, 25, 27, 28, 29, 31 bottom left, 31 top, 41, 43; Comstock: 8, 38; Penn-Plax, Inc.: 19; Peter Arnold Inc.: cover (Gerard Lacz), 2 (R. Andrew Odus); Photo Researchers: 4 (Edmund Appel), 10 (T. Bouillet), 40 (Ray Coleman), 9 (J.M. Labat/Jacana), 14 (Elizabeth Lemoine/Jacana), 33 (H. Reinhard/Okapia), 7, 17, 31 bottom right, 35, 37 (Jerome Wexler); Tony Stone Images: 42; Valan Photos: 1, 16 (Herman H. Giethoorn).